ALAN JACKSON was born in 1938 and has lived mostly in Edinburgh. He has twice attended Edinburgh University and twice left without a degree. Otherwise, apart from a period as a trainee psychiatric nurse, he has chosen to work as a labourer. Since 1961 he has given readings of his work in many places and himself published five books of poems (now all out of print), selling them largely by hand, at readings, in pubs, and elsewhere. They included *Well Ye Ken Noo*, *All Fall Down*, and *The Worstest Beast*. As secretary of the Scottish Committee of 100 he organized the 1962 sit-down against the Polaris base at Holy Loch. Alan Jackson was awarded a Scottish Arts Council grant in 1967 and is working on a book about the interaction of myth, dream and imagery in his own life and in our time. He is married and has two children.

JEFF NUTTALL was brought up in remote Herefordshire valleys. He attended various art schools, notably Corsham, and has exhibited paintings and constructions at various galleries, including Gallery One, and with Group H. He played the trumpet and piano in his own jazz band for five years, did a comic strip for *International Times*, was active with C.N.D. and the Committee of 100, and for three years produced the underground magazine, *My Own Mag*. His books include *Poems I Want to Forget*, *Come Back Sweet Prince*, *Isabel*, *Pig*, *Love Poems*, *Oscar Christ and the Immaculate Conception* and *Bomb Culture*. He has taught in secondary modern schools all his working life, at present in Norfolk; he also works in connexion with *The People Show* at Jim Haynes's Arts Laboratory. Jeff Nuttall is married and has four children.

WILLIAM WANTLING was born and raised in the American Midwest. Immediately after secondary school he saw combat in Korea in the Marine Corps and became thoroughly disenchanted with the efficacy of war to solve human problems. In 1958, due to his heroin addiction, he was committed to the California State Prison at San Quentin, where he was incarcerated for five years. He has published nine collections of poetry; his latest, *The Awakening*, has recently been published in England. William Wantling, who is married, is now working for his master's degree in English literature, and is also at work on a novel.

Penguin Modern Poets

12

ALAN JACKSON
JEFF NUTTALL
WILLIAM WANTLING

Penguin Books

Penguin Books Ltd, Harmondsworth, Middlesex, England
Penguin Books Inc., 7110 Ambassador Road, Baltimore, Maryland 21207, U.S.A.
Penguin Books Australia Ltd, Ringwood, Victoria, Australia

—

This selection first published in Penguin Books 1968
Reprinted 1969

—

Copyright © Penguin Books Ltd, 1968

—

Made and printed in Great Britain by
Western Printing Services Ltd, Bristol
Set in Monotype Garamond

Contents

CONTENTS

CONTENTS

ACKNOWLEDGEMENTS

For permission to reprint copyright material the following acknowledgements are made: for 'Mother Song' and 'Dangerous to drink day...' by Jeff Nuttall to Fulcrum Press; for poems by William Wantling to Rapp & Carroll Ltd.

ALAN JACKSON

January

Deep dark hill beauties, women's eyes,
Peaks pools and depths, penalty and prize.
O birded
   unworded
   unflown
   – known
      soul,
How deep down? What horror? What filth
Nests in my heart-hole?

Hell is
Bird under water
Fish in sky.
Hell is descent into
Under the I.

Who turned my flower
Up-down?
Blossom in mud, roots in sky?

Beauty, beauty. Who stole my ring?
What whiskers claws come in between?

I am no man. Nowt.
I fling form from me like a foe
And neither swimming crawling walking go.
Womb or mould has not been made
In which my seed stuff may be laid.

An unkind hand threw back the gates
And the beasts came in.

O my ancestors,
Who said I called? Crusty ones, bull,
Fin and wing, foot and pad,
Must I make room for you,
Human so long?
Who ate my light,
I curse.
Farewell, kind Mum and Dad,
The hairy ones have held me by the hand.

'Was a shame'

Was a shame for my mum that to make me well
I had to give her bloody hell.

She'd had the blood of my birth before
Couldn't she suffer this one more?

Far from wanting my second birth
She tried to hold me fast to the earth.

It's a pity she hadn't the heart to be glad
Her kid had guts as good as his dad.

But she hadn't and, friend, I'm no Christian fool.
I firmly believe you've got to be cruel to be cruel.

By Christ I kicked her where it hurt her most.
The noise of her screams is still my boast.

I jumped on her belly until her bones rang,
And as I jumped I danced and sang.

2

And the song I sang was of a fire
That flamed up into a bird of desire.

And the bird of desire flew in the sky
Until it turned to heaven's eye.

And heaven's eye shone in the night
And filled the earth with a birthday light.

And that birthday light was a sign for me
To leap off my mum and be free, be free.

And now, born again, no longer sick,
I kiss my mother and never kick.

'goodly godly kindly men'

goodly godly kindly men
if you pour I wont say when

wash me in the holy lather
ancient as my ancient father

scrub my toes eight nine ten
goodly godly kindly men

'Was a wee man'

Was a wee man
who lived in an egg,
sucked his own yolk,
never did beg.

Sudden one morning
set him yawning;
stretched and stroke
till the egg broke.

He ran into the world.
Air and earth skirled:
'Hooray, hurrah, he is free.
Gold and white and fighting is he'.

Our Father

Gold of the flowering sun
like an egg's been underdone
flows in to the world.
Heavenly chrysanthemum
warms our bodies like good rum
down our throats has trickled.

God divided into three
fire and flower and spirit be.

I'll love you if you'll love me.

Birth number two

Born again at twenty two
I put my foot in my father's shoe.
I'm a hook crook and comic singer
And what I crook's my little finger.

Born again at twenty two,
I've told my mumping mum to shoo.
Told her: I love you, but I love me more.
I've sucked my thumb until it's sore,
Now I'm giving it the great outdoor.

Farewell to circularity:
I'm bound for all hilarity.

Saw

I saw this nun
with a big white hat
like wings

some burd

Lord Save Us. It's The Minister.

well Mr Mackay, ye're a bonny wee man
wi yer hat pulled down over yer balls
an yer lips so tight
nothing can pass through them
                                    bar silver

yer god's a triangular monster
        a sealed length of granite
if he touched a curve, he would crumble
                                    and crash

get the hell off the surface of scotland
or i'll get the next bent moon
        to laugh you away in her tears.

Knox (1)

    the old scots grim man
            with the chin
    eats an apple on the bus

    he hides it in his pocket between bites

            for fear of the animal
            for fear of the people

Knox (2)

(second half to 'Johnny Lad')

in the pub
  where the hundred fastest women in Glasgow go
to get Americans
  I put my hand round my girlfriend's breast.
Quick as a flash the barman comes up and says:
  'Cut that out, son. This is a public bar'.

  O Knox he was a bad man
  he split the Scottish mind.
  The one half he made cruel
  and the other half unkind.
As for you, as for you, as for you, auld Jesus lad,
gawn dance the nails fae oot yer taes, an
      try an be mair glad.

Perfect

  when a christian hits the ground
  he splits in two

  one half is rotten
  and so's the other

three

sixteen months drinks the bath
quarter of a century smokes a fag
twenty's at the butcher's

the moral code

if the hair of thy neighbour offend thee
pluck it out

Young Politician

What a lovely, lovely moon.
And it's in the constituency too.

'This wifie'

This wifie wi a shoppin basket,
A goes up tae her an says
Hey wifie, see, there's the wild Pentlands
Just behind ye.

She drapped it.

Nothing

Nothing in my woman's head
didn't worry about that
Took her into C and A's
and bought her a great big purple woolly hat.

Loss

A tulip fell deid
bi ma doorstep the day
dark rid the colour o blood
Wis the only yin come up this year
A imagine it fell wi a thud

ALAN JACKSON
The Last Bad

my heart beats fast against the last bad wall
feeds its force upon the thirteenth rib
evil serums push through all my blood
the cells enact what my weird will bids

not how the flesh was meant to be used
not by the spirit subdued and bruised

there's something in the spirit can't be forgiven
icy and soaring past every sun,
earth kicking off from, except like metal,
deliberate, constructed, spun,
slender, suspended, far from home,
iron-glinted, elegant, erect,
dancing away from the body
for the big romance
with intellect

Fraulein

i am the nice german girl
i am good with children
i am good with cats
i do all the washing and the ironing
and i am leaving
i take my duffle bag and a pair of jeans and a sweater
and go for a holiday on the road

i have big breasts
what do all the men want?
what has it to do with their eyes?
only two men have seen these breasts
one stroked them and one sucked them
it was nice it was all nice
they were good to come after me
they were good to love me
but what did it mean to them?
they were so hot and tight
they were sweating
i lay and held their heads with my eyes shut
and at a certain point i did up my blouse

i am on the road
i'm not looking for a thing
i walk and sing
all the pops in american and opera in german
i get lots of lifts
some of the drivers don't speak
they buy me tea and hamburgers
and say good luck fraulein
some tell me about their families
and some always try something funny
one man got out and came round to my door

he tried to undo things
i pretended to be asleep and tossed about
he stood holding onto me and did something
to himself with his hand

in liverpool i stayed at the christian place
i took a cup a spoon and a knife
this big long car came past then past again
it stopped he was an american i got in
i didn't like him
he said he was going home after a holiday
he would put his tent for me on the beach
and come back in the morning
he didn't go away
when it got dark he lit a fire and cooked
i was awful hungry
sausages and eggs and bread and tea
then he threw some stones on the fire and grabbed me
i fought like a beast i kicked and tore him
but he was two times as big as me grunting and snarling
without words
he pressed his knees on my arms
and ripped my clothes and pulled my jeans
i was weak with hitting him
i was in a rage and crying
thinking he's mad he must be mad maybe he's got a knife
and i gave in i sank flat
he was a beast i hate him i hate men
he was like a big dagger
like being dragged by a motorbike
it was nothing to me but it was drowning me
and then i wanted something
i went with him i shouted and went up and down
                                    up and down

i hate him and i hate myself
i don't care what happens to me
i'm all hurt inside but i'm frightened to see about it
i want to have children
there's all yellow stuff
and it hurts when i go to the bathroom
he stayed all night
and the next day he drove me where i could get a lift
i never spoke to him
i would like to have killed him
men like that should be killed

Digging

fallen in a heap
again
why do i keep
falling in a heap?

i got plaster
i got bricks
i got a boxful
of tradesman's tricks
i got cement
well it's still in the bag
there isn't a tap
here that's the drag
i got sand
i got trowels
i got my dad's
good set of rules
   the architect's plan
said build a square
but i read it wrong
and built it in air
he laughed like a demon
when he saw what i'd done
said Won't last a minute
in a good-going sun
dig down there
with the help of your brutes
it won't be a square
unless it has roots
   so i dug
and i'm digging
and i'll dig

but digging's not the trouble
it's getting rid
of the rubble
he specifically said
i don't care what's done
with what you throw out of here
but we're delving to go up again
and the surface must be clear
   and here i'm surrounded
i'm mountained and mounded
with more rubbish than hole
and no barrows at all

fallen in a heap
again
why do i keep
falling in a heap?

'tiny nippled men'

tiny nippled men wander through the auld toon
in delicate high voices they cry
'we are what you're coming to'

'get away fae me, ye daft poofs'
the big drunk labourer shouts
and falls down the steps into the bog in the grassmarket

The Worstest Beast

the worstest beast that swims in the sea
is man with his bathing trunks down to his knee

the worstest beast that goes through the air
is man with his comb to tidy his hair

the worstest beast that bores through soil
is man with his uses for metal and oil

the worstest beast that hunts for meat
is man who kills and does not eat

the worstest beast that suckles its young
is man who's scared of nipples and dung

the worstest beast that copulates
is man who's mixed his loves and hates

the worstest beast that has warm skin
is man who stones himself with sin

he's the worstest beast because he's won
it's a master race and it's almost run

Out Here Now

People are dreaming the funniest dreams.
They wake in the morning to the sound of the screams,
then out to the garage and into the car
and the metal horsepower take them far

from the wife and the fire and the food and the bed
and the dragondreg memories sink back in the head.

And if that's all it was
there'd be no need to worry:
just the kids missing fairy tales
when Dad's in a hurry.

But out here now everywhere real
gun government passport cop
in darkness tension nightmare
say: Fire, fear; start, stop.

Say: 'Answer the trumpet,
huddle close,
devils exist
and they are our foes.

We don't know why
they've chosen to hate us.
But by God and his angels
they're not going to beat us.

Dig pits, build walls,
gather our friends.
We'll stamp on evil
until evil ends.'

And every man
picks another to fight,
and spends his day
massacring his night.

The Sentries

the sentries patrol the city walls
with orders
Shoot the barbarians
Watch the gates
behind them on the cool air of the night
music and light
'some lucky bastards are having fun'
(breaking glass   a shout)
to be there. . . to be one

but it would take eighty years
to buy themselves out
and in
to the barbarians

Falling

falling asleep in an armchair
lets the wind the words
rise
labourers and dons despise
the odd the weird
use fuck the pope and formulas
to keep back feared
walk in light
that's dry and tight
and wonder why the million facts
of sound and sight
won't unite
for all their thousands of boxes of tricks
that add up the info
and answer: nix
and get cheesed off
because politics
always seems to end
in opposites

and all the time a baby cries
saying feed me fill me
I'll devise
I'm warm and wet
I'm form and light
but not the light that hits the skies
I shine in dark
I shake surprise
I feed on snakes
and advertise
through dreams and art and all that's mad and terrifies
I'm here I fill

but you fear you kill
for God's sake reverse
and sprinkle me spray
I shrink I shrivel every day
self-waste and wars are my screams and cries
that your minds torch out of me
your incinerating eyes

Here

here's a magician of magnitude
my gun's a gong
my going's good
fry the females
feed the food
plant your fingers in the wood
be nude be rude
should's a prude
would's a could
biff the if
unlid the id
can the am and do the will
spend the money in the till
fuck the pope and thump the boss
the hell with profit and paper loss
drink your piss and eat your shit
wave your ballocks over it
be high be low
no yes no no
no listen no talk
muck in make mock

the clever wife puts all to use
lashings of cream and sweet fruit juice
tonsils toenails titbits stewed
hoopla
       's magic of magnitude

God

God sure wasn't
no da Vinci.
Ma feet is nice
but ma shoes
is pinchy.

Daddy

Is it true we all used to have hair on our backs?
Yes, son.
And is that why some people used to wear hair shirts
                          all the time?
No. That was for an opposite reason
   called desperate grovelling trauma.

3 l/g 4

There's leafs and pools inside to hide in
skins and pods and shells to slide in
there's barks and musk and sands to touch
lots of things in us not human very much
if we want
but we don't but only a few do
for the rest the past is mumbo hoodoo
something sucked and scaled
been transcended
a gold rush trail that's been hauled and ended

i and my self would like to sink into the non
human to the eyes
pleasure of vision the only prize
but know very well the other guys
wont give up their lust
to organize
    dissect dead flies
and get ten men working on an other man's whys
they're all at it and out
        up and on
eager to get the whole universe mapped
not sensing the pulse of their guts is gone
just as if the spinal cord had snapped
they've not felt yet they're spinning free in space
running in no race
just black
sheep shot out from home in disgrace
to make good or get lost in a distant place
to be forgotten in any case
but the signs that our minds roam on untied lines
are there in what we're wishing for

a martian year one
in our nineteen eighty four
a meeting with strange captains from a master civilization
who will bend gently over us through galactic curves
and offer what they've learned in an older universe
to help us through our long division
the conquerors of matter
and the absurds of evolution

meanwhile we discover in earth's skies at night
the unidentified flying object guilt
the beautiful round shining space ship god
the dark fast dangerous cigar shape the devil
and the appearance and eclipse in a flash of red
of three little green quarters of our personality
near an ancient burial ground just inside our head.

'reverse the pogrom'

reverse the pogrom
let the amachabites murder the jews
let the jews murder the christians
let the christians murder the CP-ites
and let them finish the job
and then like a little
lamb buried in mud
let me rise from the rubble
looking lovely in hides

Aint Gonna Be

the island of love   a nest of insects
a coloured wheel   a floating rash
a broken hand   a filthy wish
a timebuilt awkward   a fragment rumour
a frothing nark   a will-less push

underneath
                you can tell what there was
colleges ago
our mind is the boomerang prince
homes on our heads
and our gravity stretches our necks
we first fell off some thousand years
and keep in touch by eagly watching
it's not a question of going back
it's a foregone conclusion of ploughing through stone
stone is our city
we are our dead

lather our masks in the mirror
and climb into the same rigor every morning
the dead keep regular hours untouched by rain
and button their clothes against swelling
our games are based on the skeletal lurch
and our love
is the irritated mating of sea-things
in dry tanks
our wars are expected
memorize a newspaper
off a wall in pompey
and never read again
our kids are uncodeable

their ciphers fade after a year and a half
our schools are surrounded by lawns not grass

so it goes on
some things were never meant to be, jimmy
and we were one of them
the wet's going away from us all the time
and we sit dotted like currants on a dust heap of flour

aint gonna be none of that gentlefolk cake now
aint nobody left's got them malleable hands

ALAN JACKSON
The Enemies

the loyal agents of death
the general and the tight-lipped woman
remind us
to rip off our buttons
from our bellies to our throats
and dance

when death has become icy instead of hot
good men have got
to turn from the light
and use
      the drums
      the dance
      the night
to worm up the devils into the day
      and say
Ladies and gentlemen
      on our left
      and on our right
we have both the opponents at bay
and now that we've dumped the humps off our backs
      we may
      see a fair fight
and watch: for the winner won't be either of these
      but an alloy
they'll hammer out of each other tonight

Moon

they were arguing over the dead lady's body
the surgeon said
   freeze her, give me ten years
   and unlimited money
   for certain machines
   she will walk, breathe
the man from the funeral parlour said
   that is obscene
   with my hands i will give her beauty and peace
   more than is fair
   she will stay loved in the dreams
   of us trapped in air
when i hurried into the bed and said
   bells confetti priest cake
   i'm marrying future and past now
   and this is the one i take

'*tara*'

tara for now the tadpole said
and tucked his tadtail round his head
i'll sink to the bottom but i won't be dead

JEFF NUTTALL

JEFF NUTTALL

'The corkscrew worm revolves'

The corkscrew worm revolves
Writhes its iron filing twist in the soft core of
    the rock . . .

When the worm curls
Earth turns one reluctant revolution.
All the older order of the planets
Rearranges from this nuclear motor
Where the slow blind shift of the Original
    Obscenity
Performs its ancient function
Spinning out the dry husk planets
           on their stale trajectories
Needling all the silly passions
Into weeping plasma for the homo-sapiens routine.

For My Son

Mind how you go. Don't
Snap your drinking eyes so hard
You bruise the day. Don't spur the day
    to blind you.

Mind how you go. Don't
Magnify the day's electric impulse
Til your eldritch pleasure fells the halfchick sky
    to crush you.

Mind how you go. Don't
Flush such blood up to your face's measure
Pleasure's numbed in pressures
Drumming at the shut pores
    that secrete you.

Please don't
Glut your sore-pink self to show
Your flesh past dimmer glow
To edgy glister; don't let
Juices wet you like a blister running –
Like a sticky bud let lose you. Know
    the knives are out,

The blades are keen in miracle.
Your high bright sickle sheen
Could cut to stumps the You I've sown.
    Mind how you go.

'They come like a wall'

They come like a wall, stalk forward gravely,
Stalk on tall stilts, no sound, no expression,
Still advancing (though no nearer yet),
Always coming (never getting close
For some good reason.) So there's
No excuse for me to lose
A tiniest part of all their sense of menace
Even for a minute. Their continuous
Advance, whose progress never happens,
Their perpetual journey reaching no arrival
Is a constant possibility of impossible disaster,
  is unceasing threat.

Difficulty's not to overcome them
  (For we never meet . . .)
Nor to see it through with clenched teeth
  (How? It's never over.)
What I must address myself to now
Is how to live alongside the perpetual menace,
  face the stationary advance.
Not fight, nor yet defy, seek no relief
But smile towards those dolphin lips of bone
And meet those clustered berry eyes that squeak.

Notes towards a Suicide Note

Shall I tell you a secret?
You must come close
       bend very close.
You need your ear to the ground
to catch god's squeak
       sarcastic squeaking.
       I must set a trap.

Shall I tell you now
about the awful tempest
       thumping drumming
about the big and violent wind of blood
       banging up my tent of skin
to make it fat and pink?

Shall I tell you
how the wind that's drumming
at my skull of notions
pumps from the same source?
Feel the bone throb
       throb with gusty thoughts.

Should I tell you
(Don't laugh now)
that if skin burst
if the real ejaculation came

       I came

the tent would snap its guyrope.
It and I
would fly away
skull fly to feathers

hush

Not long now, my darling.
Hark at the wind.

Insomnia

Shall I do it, get up?
Go across and curl,
Curl like a hurt, furred animal?
Shall I curl like an early embryo
All hairy, simian, gone wrong?
Curl up out there, out of the bed,
Red, raw, bitten under my itch of a pelt?
All huddled up, all curled on my side?
Out of the bed and over there
Like an idiot, but I'm not an idiot,
Just a strange, shamed withered beast
Who'd whimper, there on the bedroom boards,
Whimper love,
Whimper all the limp last love away
And sleep.

Schoolmistress

In the window (sun over Totteridge trees
Throws ironic glory over her cardiganed hump) –
'Dressed in tight jeans – I threw them out.

We wouldn't have had it – not in the old days.'
Electric fire room fug and half-smoked fags
Draws out the dank sour mould of menopause.

Her eyes flash wet 'yes holding hands.
Double the school rules –
Can't tell what might go on in the cloakrooms – '
Flesh forms throb on her neck.

'Arms round each other in tight jeans – '
Sun sweat spangles her head,
Brow crowned in glistening filth – 'Yes kissing
    and so forth – '
Her knees clench, thighs move slow.

And the room-heat sun-burst 'Ought to be
    checked'
And the thick meat knicker-rut hangs in the room
' – Tight jeans – not right for school – '
Till the sun stands banners of blood in her
    swelled face
And rubs it; she rubs. 'Tight jeans . . .

Mother and Daughter

They talk. I imagine shy men, habitual voyeurs who stood on the stone step, wanker's hands clutching a rained-on trilby.

Where did they sit and how did they lie? Like me, on the edge of the Put-U-Up, a little bit over-defiant, like me in the public park, more than a little bit pissed?

And did they notice the nudges and sidelong looks, the mutual pampering mutual smoothing of midnight charms, sense the unspoken campaigns planned?

Did they wake to a blank wall just before dawn and an empty nest left warm in the sheets, to hear the purring, the sleek black blandishments out on the cold stair?

Did they creep to the door to hear the holiest secrets discussed as an old joke, then open the door, see a pair of black pedigree cats rub side to voluptuous side as they picked through the quills of a dead falcon?

Adolescence – Malvern

Muddlers murdered in deck chairs –
(Malvern lilac
Shrubs and Albert Sandler 'Songs
From the Shows') –
Wedged welded
To market-stripe deck-cloth
By sun like a stamp
Defining iron –
Dowager's boater heraldic.

White stamp sun
Sets seal on sitting stools
Of flesh pap –
Fester tropic gutter
Blossomheads of sweet putrescence –
Bursting blackhead
Varicose retirement – Glare/
Stamp/Signature on stick-limbs:
'Property Of Afternoon.'

Lace-&-summer-muslin hung
Attendants – lavender
Deaths' heads. Gums
Clamped, jaws clamped on gums;
Sun holds the whole,
Bright pliers pinching pap in place –
Attendants on a child

Who learns his lesson well:
'The swarming maggots in the rose
Betray your waking flesh
– Remember that!' sings

Catgut whine of Desert Song and
    Chocolate Soldier
And the Merry Widow always there
Stock-still and lilac-shrouded in the
    shrubbery.

Summer drops dollars

Summer drops dollars. They land flat –
Dark discs on thirsty asphalt.
My apparition prays in Manor Road
Waiting in its daft disguise of body.
Privet, laurel, maggot-nibbled rose blooms
Curdle their respective masses, seething
    textures,
Hungry tribes for the first coins.
They snap them up jealously –
Lizard lips trapping a fly.

In the female steam, hot perfume from the
    avenues
    (Woman's Hour music from a distant bay) –
In the afternoon vat where sick vegetation
Comes to the boil in a tight silence
My ghost lifts a head like a rotting rose
Sucking the samples as vegetation sucks
But waiting for the ultimate flush
When the brimful bucket of suspended storm
Spills down the sticky entrails of the flowers
And gardens open wide as women, gasping.

Sunsets

Youth, then yawning hunger, wanted to walk there,
Had a yen that settled nowhere lower than the molten
    place –
Wade about in all that yolk, that evening drift.
Yenned to suck sour all the shifting red clouds,
Tattered bandages of old dead heroes draped to dry.

Never made it, naturally. Who does?
Who does anything but wait (you wait a long time too)
Wait watching on the right night
Light like orange peel on house façades
All down one side of any street – bay window bonfires –
Watch valhalla washline strung across the chrome,
Sun swum in grease, a fat fried egg?

Who does anything but wait till the protector comes,
That righteous little shit, the one that dragged you down
                    dreary with his drab pattern?
Who paddles in the sunset save he –
              (Watch it! He's waddling this way)
Slash all oils of the bastard's brain
To curdle where the coloured clouds show clear –
(Dig that one, shepherd, How's that for a glow?)
Stir crude evening smashed to smear, wild
Whorls in gutter glue? Then hold my hand a bit.
I'll give you gold where we're going now.

'Open my bones'

Open my bones when the rain spills
Slops from the slits in suspended gasbubs
Hovering over the sea.

The pregnant twelve-year scrubber
Was hung from the pier on her own black nylon –
Sits along the skyline with the other bloated objects
   (apricots . . .).

The wincing sergeant wrung the thunderheads
   paraded on the world's edge, fruit along a mantel
   mellowing,
Grabbed them grasped in his greasepalm –
Juice in your eye – suck rain . . .

I put out my eyes. The sockets were buckets.
Daggerjuice dug in the optic nerve.
My head sang back a soundless thanks
Through my sockets my sockets, the bone gob
Vomiting flocks of feathered apricots.

Radiomessages shot up the vertical rain in a shock
   chain,
Mind for the dead girl shot from my brain.
Stretch out your thin limbs hard for the dropped god.
Your pellet of red released to the fall of the storm
Is here in my head so listen, I'm speaking its voice.
Weather skull uterus, fleshlobe grown in a bone cave
So trust me. I'll tend him with pain.

Lucifer

Screaming: 'I'm eagle.'
Sucking brown sweets: 'I'm the wide span' (cheek
    on tattered chiffon.)
'Rubies, dew from entrails
Sheath my hebe beak: I'm the heights . . .'

Blood soured.
Buboes broke crowns
Crying lost kingdoms of love.
With the tide swabbed (soft song hovering talons),
Tongue dry, dawn a waste cast smeared on the win-
    dow
Look at the rooster
Yahweh's mad bantam
Spread up the gutter sky.

The Twin*

The visitors came in a flood on Sundays
                         walked down the ward
Bristling their bags and bouquets and bottles
Of Lucozade Lemonade Robinson's
                         Barley Water
Festooned with daffodils
Daft with their better-dear smiles.

And always the smiles turned uncertain
On passing the big bed made to seem vast
By the tininess –
          Sliver of wide-eyed black-eyed
Night-hair child – Smiles soured at her terrible eyes
               Black windows on a whole quick cosmos
               Wet windows on comets
                    Crash silent in a velvet everywhere.
And one woman stopped spoke smiled
But never a word and the universe churned in the eyes.

And a pink man stopped with a sweet
And held it and left, unthanked and unanswered,
Leaving the sweet on the table.
It lay three days. The night nurse nicked it.

Another child, come with mum,
Left his family, crept to the bed,
Looked solemn through the solemn eyes for five full
   minutes.
Then ran for the exit in tears.

* It sometimes happens that children are born with their own
twin inside them in the form of a cyst.

And the visitors went and the evening meal
Passed by and at night
In the creaking, whimpering dark
The systems turned in the pebble of head
And the voices came that she mustn't repeat . . .

I shall not tell them
          The planets screamed in their gas
They mustn't know
          The big air breathed through her solemn interior
          voids
That they cut from my toddler's tummy my dead twin
Brother they hacked from my belly was hair and had
          hands like flowers
And they mustn't know that I haven't the words
And they mustn't know that I know that the words aren't
          coined
For everything that my body knows
That there isn't the loneliness big enough
To encompass the self that's left behind
That when later I walk out in womanhood where
Can the love or the man be to honour the yearning wound
Where the ultimate horror of love lay curled in sleep
That they scooped out, slopped in a bucket of Dettol and
          flushed?

In The Park

(from the novelette 'The Case of Isabel and the Bleeding Foetus')

The stars were public flowers, leaning tall stalks, watching; public flowers were stars.
The flowers were secretaries civil servants clerks inspecting me, their stalks like legs of secretary birds.
The bird-beaked people, come to see and ask, were glare – accusing mass of stars.

The starlight was a floodlight desklight glare interrogation light.
The light apocalypse sent beams that glanced around my guilty pelvic bone.
The shadowkilling Christlight dried the blood to scum across my face.

The mad stars knew me, knew the reason you were weeping.
Flowerlens lamps flashed spectacles with sunflower lenses.
Watched my wish to gnaw the sweet vagina from you, tear your kind cling out in ribbons, spit it in their secretary faces.

Morning – when I telephoned – thank Christ there you were, okay. I hadn't really done it.
They knew though, yes they know, the bright inquisitors on tall stalks watched the whole damn operation, shrilling anthems.

'Driving the jumper'

Driving the jumper, the leaping thing, bucking bright
    impulse,
Driving the nails that are dragging it down
In the sticky dip of the bone bowl. Breydon
                'S a metal map.
                Breydon's a water of lead.
                Breydon's a graveyard for the sky.

My snake leaps thrashing cockwhip up against the sky-
    lead. Sparks.
                – the lead of the nothing the nothing
                the nothing . . .

If I bend far enough over my tea in the harbour caff
Fat folds of gut will buckle down gladness – Spit out the
    tea and the lady says 'Are you alright?'
Can't let it out. Must make it cut me, my cave-mind, my
    stomach pink,
Red network of trickling grasscuts – legs
Running over the fields. . .

Not for your tallow throats, you earlydawn scrubbers.
You climb from your lilac dreams, go to the businessface
    office; you're safe.
Scrubbers or trembling mice, you're safe from a nip of
    the giggling heartbroken viper. Hand
In my pocket – my snake is a separate mover, my snake a
    usurper. *I'm very much afraid not.*

The sky is myself and myself is lead and myself crushes
    down on the soft soft neck of summer. I'll eat it.

It's a secret. You're safe – hot gem/melt pearl/gone gob
    of energy.
It's prisoned palmed.
It'll poison my pocket.
The metal will kill down your dangerous prayers.

I am lead I am metal.
The anvil is all of the law.

'Blood let'

Blood let/melt light/apple bleed/catch sun
Sun late, gurgling in its westerly mess,
They run out, shrieking geese across the
    darkening, the dead girls.

I don't want to look at the cuts on her arms.
I've an eyeful of glass I've a headful of metal.
I'm cool, baby, cool, okay, I keep telling you.

Child on glass candlesnot grief
Dirty cut/Pain of the rough cold flannel/No
    soap

– Hysterical, used a blunt blade.
– Only said 'God if you're there if you're
– Yes if you're there you can fuck my cuts.
Listen. My mouths. My imprisoned selves . . .'
                    There was once a young summer who
                    kept her family of mongol selves well
                    fed through cuts for mouths like un-
                    lipped prickholes. Feed . . .

feed feed feed.
Summer's a bounty of long dead pregnancies.
What can the thunder do when it comes
But heighten the green of the poison?

Thunder volt be still.

Lead for me.

Metalbody.

To My Wife

Jesus Christ nailed to the tree by a mob of bad soldiers
  bent over

                    Grimacing (Flemish Room
                        at the National Gallery.)
David's idea and he must have felt it –
Felt, like you, block in the bone of his head, the rock of
  a feeling,
Dead, cold boulder of *loneliness* looking from eyes (riveted)
                        Of Christ (nailed)
Hammer the visitors – follow the poor sods riveting
                    riveting all round the gallery
                        The way Mona Lisa's
                            supposed to.
Christ out of you by old Painter David in some pass out
  of time

                    (Both of you laying aside from
                        the centuries)

That's how he made the brush give image
How he defined your painful sainthood
Worn in your womb a small white flower
Worn in your eyes glass rocks, flash pain – nails ham-
  mered accusing
Brash shafts clanging: 'Why are you doing this to me
                    and what are you going to do next?'

JEFF NUTTALL

'*An ancient thing*'

An ancient thing
Purity covered in silt of the centuries
One cry at climax cracks the deposit
Tears burst through
Clear springs in April fields – as cruel

The first god
Wrapped in the fat of long feeding
Stained underthings crusts of the birthbed
Sewn up in scars – the zipper signs of forced
    deliveries
Womanstink torn down the front
Shows a daisy flower wondering why at
    the light

The deepest cave
Rich as a farmyard with wear of its usage
As whorehouse and cradle and drain
The stiff growth parted
Fumble through lips oiled with the leavings
    of living
To find the ultimate tunnel
Fresh as the babies that passed
And the wondering eyes.

'Hide and seek'

Hide and seek – spoor trails in and out of the brain
    woods –
Hide a brain around the ghost boles of the tall ash.
Look out my giggling love
The skull snake stands at your shoulder o hissing its
    venomous carols.
Spoor trails out of the giggling love –
Ghost snake hissing its venom . . .

I put my hands in the worm cascade the waterfall worms
    of hair
Oh show me your little pink shame
The pink knot clitoris shame that you speak through
Breaking your black teeth to crumbs in your mumbling
    muscle
The working head; needle pain travels hot comets
Into the sore strained core of your shoulder hump.
Serpent glad, horn mouth grinning its carols – black
    crumbs little pink worms and the working needle.

Came on you later in the game; you stood some way off.
It was evening, the serpent against you.
Poured yes you poured your shadowed flesh over his
    penis of fishbone ribs skull helmet
Like leaves like the falling gestures of trees that are dying
You poured self. I stood in the evening and watched.
Whistle and off I said – evening against your blue flesh –
    fishbones like falling self – serpent, his penis of trees.

Catch me he's with me.
Burst if you can through thickets of guilty hair.
He's with me now, singing his hush
While my bruised mouth open for pain, pleads forgive-
      ness,
Is poised out of contact an inch from his quivering fish-
      head.
The grey smoke lost to the trees is yours
You open for contact
You poised out of bruised forgiveness.

The Whore of Kilpeck*

Who'd couple with foetus, with handful of sore yell wet,
    with its jelly eyes staring,
Clamped round the grunt-root sucking it up to a rash?

The Mother of Red Muck slewed out her gibbering
    sheelaghnagig.
The entire spring season ploughed her in her eldritch
    luminous paralysis.

Who'd help her or give to her further? She squats and she
    claws clamp-hands at her loud wet seed-pit. The
    hazel twigs whimper.

She is old in stone. She was dropped from the earth's
    womb three months early, ejaculated by the violence
    of her own imprisoning desire.
The stone is her desire. The ancient permanence has made
    her always now.
Who could acknowledge or deny her carolling berserk
    thirst?

The stone season whimpers loud beneath the sward.
Will some one for Christ's sake soon stand keen as the
    sharp Welsh metal in the streaming slough and hack
    the year to winter?

* On the Parish Church of St Mary and St David, Kilpeck,
Herefordshire, is a small Celtic fertility figure made up of head
and hands which are holding open a huge vagina. It is called by
the local people the Whore of Kilpeck.

'I stalk with the razorblade cranes'

I stalk with the razorblade cranes, my pinhead reeling
    wingpower in the white light,
Stilt legs reed legs red from menstrual delta.
I stalk with an agate eye and a lunatic trapped in my
    fossilized head – My stare . . .

My feathers are all the flash, the flash the dawn and finish.
    I am not outside the instant Being-Scream.
My pride is everywhere. I'm proud because the every-
    where is me.

The lunatic is in my skull – his blazing replica is spat out
    molten on the dying sky.
I walk a while, a long while I walk. The instant's constant.
    Something in me won't die. Help me.

Sun Sequence

1

Stalks down with his scythe
Swings down the corn-bread sky –
Buttered cob of a stalk-on – wet sweat
Myriad image of himself –
Flash galaxies across him.
Lips rich spit and big-light teeth –
Long hook locked in everybody's
Yearning crotch releasing love gum
– Song of scared stoat . . .
Hacks out cream screams up the sky
Stretched rodent throat ejaculating
Semen of his stopped life
Floods   Joy   Blind   White

2

I shake to the violent light
                    shaft fall flood
                    vertical drop
                    cruel column
                    sun's bile
                    white shiner

Two columns: God   Frail
             Ghost   upright
             Sun   Daft trashpile
             Shaft   Man's bonerack
Stand edge to edge
Self shakes lily liver leaf
Next to the daydrop
            sunsuck
            vicious vacuum pull

That sinks you to sockets of rock
Or sucks you to scorch in the governor's vulcanized grin.

3

At every day's grey
My creaking neck's tested.
I twist back my joints
My lustframe arched.
Knobs squeak pelvic sockets.
I grind my vertebrae
Testing ligament.
Head turns slow slow
Slow like the turn
Of the world.
Scalp on the pillow, neck
Sprung for the sacrifice arch.
Mouth open.
I wince up my eyes
Open thighs
And my anus
For noon
The hot sod
With his bells
And his blade.

4

First blade
Sweet sting
Skull to crotch
Gut worm
In the cold air. Suck

Wire iron
For eyesockets
Brains on my face
Snails for the bull's
Bright tongue
Armature scraped down
With razors and scoops
White shock
Bone through the pink
Clean   Clean

Heart hot
Sweetmeat
Hung hooked
Brain-swathed
Old thoughts
Flown from
Chopping chopping
Singing soon –
I'm gone.
There's One.

Lightening Sequence

I

Centre shaft quivers the lightening down to the roots –
      (– Walk on your roots –)
And the charge of the earth sap, the wet clay hydro spins
    it back up
And the lightening stabs it back down – charge of white-
    flame tingling
Down urethral throat – whole body and spirit a crucial
    erection
Singing metal struck muscle of weather breath –
(What lightening in the leaves
What fire lice to cluster curdling into one another's
    crevices
Sap-gum-clung to one-another's flat discs)
Suck the leaves yes suck them
Into the eyes of your yawning column
Watch SPLASH salt spunk running down the shattered
    glass
Of the dome where the noon burned.
The light and the heat
        will lick me dry of my day salt ...

And the agony thank you oh thank you
I spurt up the sun – grows fat
Splits pomegranate seeds spill – (catch them)
Suck suck leaf and seed oh fat fruit
Lemon razor walking shit like gust of hot rain.

II

Gold   Gold   Gold
Fruit light   Love buttocks
And the delicate animal fold of the yellowgirl flesh

Crease musk
Cave smells centuries of stale air
Cathedrals   Catacombs
Lost in wilderness where nonetheless surely
Too many people breathed too long and too long ago
Tombs and the tight kind mouth
Between the folding moons . . .

Lean planets in sleek action –
Interlocked spheres and the loosejointed stilts –
The polestar cracks a fingerjoint.
What night sky smells of sleep and tobacco?
No sky has a mouth so kindly tight.
There's a thin-lipped haven. Tongue like a fat god
Hugged in diurnal buttocks . . .

Man's milk shot glad cataracts
Fading light smiles and glare grins
Flashing up the airwalks corridors of force and
     black black black

III

I love you for your piston rhythm
Clam sharp rocks of granite up your garden
Drink your humus loam slime web my tongue with
     ancient snail cream –
Rainbow trails on clay – the growth the tickling growth
     the night . . .

I fuck you skies and every season peels back petals thrust-
     ing out
wet entrails that weep cream and the thick spring showers.
I hail you – punishing stones of glass

Fuck your sad pool eyes with a sharp cruel drumming of
 the season – dimples deep reflections –
Handfulls of fat flowers shat from the stained holes
Massed round my straining praying gland in posies of kiss
 and forgive.

I could shriek you and weep you I fuck you love
All tears turn firecracker thunderstorm
Flash up your ridgeway and burn down the frail black
 fronds of your fuckhole hair
Black wet black green nightbreath rustle garden-cunt
 black
And the morning the morning the slow pearl poised on
 the world's fat gland and the peace.

WILLIAM WANTLING

The Awakening

I found the bee as it fumbled about the ground
Its leg mangled, its wing torn, its sting
    gone
I picked it up, marvelled at its insistence
    to continue on, despite the dumb brute
    thing that had occurred
I considered, remembered the fatal struggle
    the agony on the face of wounded friends
    and the same dumb drive to continue
I became angry at the unfair conflict suffered
    by will and organism
I became just, I became unreasoned, I became
    extravagant
I observed the bee, there, lying in my palm
I looked and I commanded in a harsh and angry shout –
    STOP THAT!
Then it ceased to struggle, and somehow suddenly
    became marvellously whole, and it arose
    and it flew away
I stared, I was appalled, I was overwhelmed
    with responsibility, and I knew not where to begin

For Lennie Bruce, for Us

the world soon kills
what it cannot suffer
you went the way of
all shining things
  yet
     perhaps
to approach the final peace
of overdose
& find the courage to pass beyond
  is also why
you burned so bright in life
Yes Man, we dug
the wild Jew Tiger, knew
the cindered ash must fall

  between
yesterday's 7 San Francisco hills
 &
today's last grasping gasp
for one short brilliant moment
burned tomorrow's stars

WILLIAM WANTLING

'without laying claim'

without laying claim
to an impossible innocence
I must tell you how
in the midst of that crowd
we calmly pulled the pins
from six grenades
mumbling an explanation
even we didn't believe
& released the spoons
a lump in our throats

Pusan Liberty

the 6 × 6 bounces me down the
washboards roads, I see the

sun-eaten walls of Korea, my
girl-wife & child in a mud &

straw hut back in Taegu & here
I am meeting the SEAL as he

sits on his roller-skate cart
minus arms & legs but beneath

his ass a million $'s worth
of heroin – I make my buy

walk through the 10,000 cam-
era market-place, jeeps for

sale, people for sale, I'm
even for sale as I find the

porch of Cutie's suckahatchi
house & fix, sitting in the

sun on the adobe veranda, the
2 Chinese agents come around

to make their buy, 2 young
boys, they're hooked bad & I

charge them too much – we sit
there & fix, I fix again, the

so-called Enemy & I, but just
3 angry boys lost in the immense

absurdity of War & State sudden
friends who have decided that

our hatred of Government exceeds
the furthest imaginable limits

of human calculation.

Initiation

What were we doing, being
    cool?
That argument Kitten, on
    the freeway
I couldn't keep up our
    habits and
We cruised along sick,
    seeking magic
And you said – Hit some
    chump over his head
But I didn't dig that so
    you offered
To find some good tricks

I got hot, indignant like
    a square with tears
And you felt pity, saying

– Don't cry Daddy, it's just
another way to burn a sucker

Poetry

I've got to be honest. I can
make good word music and rhyme

at the right times and fit words
together to give people pleasure

and even sometimes take their
breath away – but it always

somehow turns out kind of phoney.
Consonance and assonance and inner

rhyme won't make up for the fact
that I can't figure out how to get

down on paper the real or the true
which we call life. Like the other

day. The other day I was walking
on the lower exercise yard here

at San Quentin and this cat called
Turk came up to a friend of mine

and said Ernie, I hear you're
shooting on my kid. And Ernie

told him So what, punk? And Turk
pulled out his stuff and shanked

Ernie in the gut only Ernie had a
metal tray in his shirt. Turk's

shank bounced right off him and
Ernie pulled his stuff out and of

course Turk didn't have a tray and
caught it dead in the chest, a bad

one, and the blood that come to his
lips was a bright pink, lung blood,

and he just laid down in the grass
and said Shit. Fuck it. Sheeit.

Fuck it. And he laughed a long
time, softly, until he died. Now

what could consonance or assonance or
even rhyme do to something like that?

'*All the fucking time*'

All the fucking time
I was in San Quentin
I kept remembering my
stinking bitch of an
old lady and how I'd
rode the beef for her
and how she'd stopped
writing in 9 months
and served papers and
shacked up with some
Chicano from East L.A.
who was a pimp & on
parole from Q himself
and let me tell you
Jack, it was *good* to
lie there in my top
bunk while my cellie
snored & think of all
the ways I'd *do* them
when I hit the streets
and I tell you Jack IT
GOT SO GOOD TO ME I MORE
THAN ONCE *COME* behind
it – then after 5½ years
I got my date then 2 weeks
later I got the letter
from my Chick's mother
saying You remember
how Shirley & you caught
Hepatitus off that dirty
needle, well she got it
again somewhere and I

don't know quite how to
tell you this but last
Tuesday at 7 pm she died
in L.A. General Hospital
and the Public Assistance
people has placed your
son in a Foster Home and
want you to sign Adoption
papers . . .
Like I've been on the bricks
almost 6 months now and tried
it with about 10, 12 chicks
and can't cut the mother –
fucking mustard Shit I wonder
what's wrong?

In the Enemy Camp

It looks as if I'm to
spend my life in enemy
camps. 2 months ago I
finally got free of San
Quentin and the Calif
Dept of Corrections –
after 5½ years. So I
came to Peoria to free-
load and Write. Now for
2 months I haven't heard
Art Pepper or Gerry
Mulligan or Jimmy Guiffre
– not even on the radio
Farmer Bill but no Charlie

Mingus or John Handy. To-
day I got funny looks when
I walked around town in
my go-aheads. The whore-
houses have been closed
since 1953 and when I
offered to eat a girl
up she looked shocked
and asked me if I've
seen a doctor about my
sex problem. The boys
don't play my game
either. I can't find
one lousy joint of weed
and nobody here ever
heard of Peyote. The cops
are polite and the negroes
humble. I'm thinking of
moving on. How far to
the next enemy camp?

'just lately'

just lately
I've seen through it
I've seen through it all
once, you know
I was quite religious
but now
there is nothing, nothing

yet still I pray

O Nothing, that
which is Cipher, which
is Naught
please
do not slay me with your
drab despicable days of
loss, of dumb terror
fulfilled, of pain . . .

You!   Peasants!
        you can't
know how much I need
to laugh
        how badly I only
    want   to   laugh

& what if the dam should
suddenly burst
If suddenly I should run
headlong, frothing, haphazardly
hurling shrapnel grenades
into high-noon crowds?

if suddenly tossing aside
the dead ugly ache of it
all, I equalled the senseless
with my brute senseless act?

O My, wouldn't I
shine?   wouldn't
I shine then?
wouldn't it be *I* then who
had created God
at last?

A Theory of Love

Baby you knew that
love was swinging
and that it made you
high and it was meant

to burn with a brief
consuming flame and

there should be nothing
left after to cry out or

beg forgiveness or
rise from the ashes

seeking to be born
again but what you

didn't know was that
you couldn't consume

me totally because of
the icecold rock at my

center which was the
form the ashes took

when they were ashes
of a very small child

whose flame had burnt
brilliantly at the age

of three when his bitch
of a mother had left

him alone in his bed
after warming it with

her whispers and her
promises and her hot

cloying presence just
before the end of it

all became the ever
repeated beginning . . .

It's Cold for August

it's cold for August
& it's been raining now
for 3 days & nights
a vague unease has
settled over many in
this place
        unease
denied in the usual
manner, things going
on as usual

  when I see
the people playing
golf in a Sunday rain
  see them
flocking to a small
sad circus & being
gaily cheated, peeping
small sad peeps of
counterfeit joy, as if
the grand old days had
  never ended
        or I
notice the insects are
gone, the ladybugs
  the lightning bugs
  the grasshoppers &
    the ants
& how few birds
returned this year

I remembered the famed
mount of ancient days, how
the volcano came like the
    Voice of God, burying the
town as it went about
its daily tasks
& then remember the
Hiroshima volcano, the
one erupting over
    Nagasaki
& I walk alone through
a deserted park, wishing
I could leave with the
birds, or like the black
dog before me, pissing
on the nearest public
statue

The Weapon

I was making it on this beach
in northern washington &
my partner sam walked the summer sands
with this sign

SEE THE GENUINE BEATNIK

i blew my bongos for the lames &
they dropped quarters
in a little cup that said

POT FUND

when the cup was full &
the sun had set &
all the lames had gone home
we melted down the quarters &
cast silver bullets in the sand &
snuck into their homes & shot them

Who's *Bitter?*

when Judge Lynch
denied probation
& crammed that 1 – 14
up my ass
for a First offence
I giggled

when Dr God
stuck 7 shocktreatments
to me
for giving my chick
in Camarillo
2 joints
I laughed aloud

now
when the State of Illness
caught me bending over
2 jugs of Codeine
cough medicine
& charged me w/Possession
& Conspiracy
I shrieked
in idiot joy

a bit worried
they all inquired
– What are you Wantling?
– A goddam Masochist?
I, between hilarious gasps
O howled – No,
– I'm a Poet!
– Fuck me again!

Conversation upon Brushing Against The Taut Form of a Susceptible Stranger on a Crowded City Bus

– How lovely! As
if, she sd
– The power of love were
not dead
        but dormant
. . . and you
the imp of my longing
flesh
        had found
my strength and bathed
it in our sudden flowing
           juices

– Where do you get off? I sd
visions
      of endless
cock-balls in my head

– At Paradise, but
nowhere now
         for
Paradise is
where we are
          she sd
lying down, inviting
me with sweet
obscene gestures . . . then
softly sobbing as I
      fled

WILLIAM WANTLING

Goodbye Porkpie Hat
– for Charlie Mingus

goodbye Fix on saturday night
when Fat Mama slips me a Dime
goodbye long lemon & white port swill
for the bone-ache days ahead & behind

goodbye Laws I can't afford
& litigation 10 years long
long's the white man rides the bench
of Law's a double-edged sword

Yeh! goodbye backdoor blues
at the restaurant carries *The Label*
if I can't eat with you fine folks
I'll chop the legs off your table

Yeh! goodbye jailhouse grey & blue
for just holding Weed one time
Aw, goodbye ol' Porkpie Hat
I had enough of you

& goodbye Harlem's Uncle Tom
rat in the corner, he spits, somehow
but nobody wants his corner, Nah
it's the nasty one, the sad one, now

& goodbye white man's god
& goodbye that Fool allah too
it's always Power they wants
& they steals that Power from *you*

I'm my own Law Man – fuck over me
I'm gonna *Act* now, not sing Blue
Aw, goodbye Porkpie Hat
I *sure* had enough a you

The Death of Caryl Chessman

Little did i know, then
The price of my revenge
If someone had foretold
Those long years of quiet
    terror and grey steel
I would have shrugged and
    laughed, saying
'A hard price for having my
    way with a virgin.'
Then the long years began
And setting aside my hot
dreams of glory
I came to understand . . .

So they bathed my body with
    gas

For a Nordic Child

You are a cold northern woman from a cold
northern land, a dark land, windy & wild
with mist-shrouded cliffs and constant
hunger where the wolves howl from snow-
torn ledges. I see your ancestors, the
race of blond ones that sprang from strange
distant places. The Cro-Magnon hunches
over a small fire in the crevice of a cliff.
He rips his meat in blood chunks & searches
an early dusk with grey falcon eyes. A
stir in the cave behind him catches the
corner of his eye & he sees again the
lush virgin being prepared for the Old Man
of the tribe. Her golden hair is being
greased & braided by the old crones, but
she smiles cunningly at the fire-watcher
Her eyes are blue. She licks her lips &
it is the meat she smiles for, the antici-
pation of it, warm and blood-odored. But
the fire-watcher, young, stronger than any,
has another hunger. Power is his goad, &
lust, now that his cruder hunger is appeas-
ed. He moans in back of his throat & rises,
yellow-furred form hunched, holds the warm
juiced chunk of meat before him & approaches
the rear of the cave. The crones have seen
this happen before. They scurry away. The
girl smiles again, victoriously, reaches
out for the warm odored offering & tears it
with her small, sharp, milk-white teeth as
the fire-watcher pushes her down & takes
her there on the rock strewn ground. When

this tale has reached the Old Man & he
roars his anger down upon them, the fire-
watcher kills him in sudden crushing combat & *his* power is born. These were your
ancestors. This is you, now, with layer
upon layer of concepts added. And it fas-
cinates me.

'a plea for workmen's compensation for t. monk'

to make up for t. monk
to take the place of t. monk
to hold sway on t. monk
to make way for t. monk
to ask grace for t. monk
make peace with t. monk
make a place for t. monk
trade places with ol' monk
trade faces with ol' monk
lake day labor – tabor bore maybe
born for thelonious monk

> a scotch physic on former busy
> thelonious monk
> take a cue from
> blow the blue drum
> say the gay song
> play the gay dog
> do not deny for i love you monk

cador drey tune
> slow flow day soon
> > neighbor day for nay day
> > labor again the flavor

table blessing never lessing congo blessing
blessings on you Great & Glorious Monk
creative day for coming way out
all you little monks
BLAH
? where's your soul monk ?
plink plank plunk
monk cant funk
wheres
your
soul
thelonious
m
o
n
k
?
maybe
charlie mingus has it

'and children are born'

and children are born
with deep eyes
and grow up
and die
knowing nothing
feeling little
but pain
and it continues
all go their ways
all ways the same

without change
birth
death
and in between
little but
deep wondering eyes
and pain

Oh, the bitter grows sweet
and the sweet bitter
and paths run through the grass
and towns are here and there
and trees, and often
lakes, birds
and always the wind blows
the sun rises
always too
the deepeyed children
forget, age into eyes
of glass, of stone
tumble the void
blind, dumb, alone
and always
nothing
always
pain

Lemonade 2c.

Kathy was my
first customer
naturally, I
turned her on
free
she put her
cool hand in
mine
led me to her
dark & sweaty
cellar
kissed me
Lord, how our
lips trembled
how bitter-sweet
& cool
that lemonade

Aesthetics

it was a strange Eden
hardly a paradise
but the best we had

Sam chortled & threw oranges
   at poets
while Bob tumbled headlong
through the grass, threw poems
at Sam, & shouted
– Look, look at me!
Mort sneered & strummed
while Jennifer danced, supple
   as a wooden stake
Ruthie prattled of Bill, while
Bill looked wise & eyed
   the horizon
waiting for Snake

Then, as always
Eve showed
cuddled them each alone
snatched the apple
   from Tom
(who had turned to stone)
& tossed it in the air

when it came down
Bob was there
Bill found Snake
Jennifer turned to flame
Tom got stoned

Ruthie prattled
Mort strummed
Sam threw oranges

but it wasn't the same

Once

there was
birth, death
beginning, & end
identity, diversification
coming into existence
& passing from it

Now
there is
nothing
absolute void
inexhaustible
without end
unmoving
without a path
a zero
where
all things are not touched
all sounds are not heard
empty
naked
still

silent
deserted
pure

Now

'at the market-place'

at the market-place
we sell many things
including love & courage
but these you must bring
    with you
& pay for as you leave

The Question Is

– You   Pig-Rat, the
Warden sd
– You think yr slick, but
there's another 5 thousand
just like you
out on the Big Yard
We'll get you, we
get 'em all, sooner
or later
What makes you think
yr special– What makes
you think we won't get
you? heh heh
Snuffle heh umm . . .

– You won't get me, Warden
cause I'm *not* like those
others on the Big Yard
I pity you, you poor squirming
bundle of nerves, I pity
you – *but they hate you*
& pity isn't careless
Hate is

It was worth 10 days
in The Hole to see
his face whiten, his
lips tighten & tremble
More than worth it
The question is, did
they get me?

San Quentin's Stranger

In death Row's dim undersea
light, he watched them
preparing the Pellet, testing
the cables & pullies, & it
held his terror of the dawn

He read again
her last letter
& knew his last bond
with life
was this memory
of a girl's cool hand

During the next hour
a chaplain came
to offer an empty hope
But he would not allow
that futile prayer, that
wasted hour

In the last half-hour
his despair shifted
& in that slight pivotal
point he embraced
the life which consumed him
found there was no fate
he could not surmount
with scorn

Heroin

what
I remember of the good times . . .

high, once I ate 3 scoops of icecream
high it was the greatest
    greater than the Eiffel tower
    greater than warm sex, sleepy
    early on a morning

    and once, high . . .
so high I never reached that peak
again, happy my wife & I
lie coasting beside a small pond
in an impossibly green park
under a godblue sky
birds swimming V's on the smoky water
the sun weaving patterns through the
leaves, small shadows swimming on
her face & arms
& she says – Baby, I feel so *fine*.

so fine . . .
that was twice
the rest was nothing, even
less
the pain's still there

For a Girl Who Doesn't Like Her Name

You are young and slender and sitting straight
in the seat as you peer at me over the edge of
    your glass
– Call me Kim, you say
– I think Camille sounds so silly.

O Baby you don't know how good Camille sounds
    to this poor simple poet
Camille   Camille   Camille   Camille

How it runs over my tongue like butter and honey
and how it calls out to the butter of your hair
and the cream and honey of your long full legs
and the cool look on your tangerine lips

(To really get crude Baby, how it goes with
    drool
    and
    fruit)

Camille   Camille   Camille   Camille
(Cream Honey Butter Fruit Drool Camille
    Hoo!
        Ha!
           Oboy!
               I'm a dog)

But wait – even poets can be serious – it's
    permitted once in a while
Don't you know Baby, how your legs will change
and the butter will run out of your hair and
    the cream and honey will leave you

Even the cool tangerine lips will lose their
    cool smile
You'll grow old and none will remember you as
    I see you now
Unless they can let Camille Camille Camille
run over their tongues and know as I know
when I hear it how you once were and how
it sounds and looks and smells to me now

Time and the City
Some Seventeen Syllable Comments

1

On the freeway
I follow redglow taillights
To my city of glass

2

I was not here yesterday
also
I will not be here tomorrow

3

Will you please explain this
I hate you
I fear you
I return always

4

The pain of your people
tears my flesh
Still . . .
There is the hour before dawn

5

I will not be here yesterday
also
I was not here tomorrow

1
2
3
4
5
6
7
8
9

WILLIAM WANTLING